Jill Dawett-Dunn

The Keys,
Witney
Oxon
PAGE 18

VOICES OF TODAY

Edited by Natalie Nightingale

First published in Great Britain in 2002 by Poetry
Today, an imprint of
Penhaligon Page Ltd, Remus House, Coltsfoot Drive,
Woodston, Peterborough. PE2 9JX

© Copyright Contributors 2002

All rights reserved. No part of this publication may be
reproduced, stored in a retrieval system, or transmitted
in any form or by any means, without prior permission
from the author(s).

A Catalogue record for this book is available from the
British Library

ISBN 1 86226 644 1

Typesetting and layout, Penhaligon Page Ltd, England.
Printed and bound by Forward Press Ltd, England

Foreword

Voices Of Today is a compilation of poetry, featuring some of our finest poets. This book gives an insight into the essence of modern living and deals with the reality of life today. We think we have created an anthology with a universal appeal.

There are many technical aspects to the writing of poetry and *Voices Of Today* contains free verse and examples of more structured work from a wealth of talented poets.

Poetry is a coat of many colours. Today's poets write in a limitless array of styles: traditional rhyming poetry is as alive and kicking today as modern free verse. Language ranges from easily accessible to intricate and elusive.

Poems have a lot to offer in our fast-paced 'instant' world. Reading poems gives us an opportunity to sit back and explore ourselves and the world around us.

Contents

A Moment In Time	Elizabeth Higgins	1
We're English	Pauline Brown	2
Chloroform Crescendo	Vann Scytere	3
The Snowman's Lament	Cherry Lea Lawton	4
Deep In Our Hearts	Myra Selvadurai	6
Together	Adele C W Crane	7
Heartache	Peggy Johnson	8
Dreams Part 3	Chris T Barber	9
The World At Peace	Dorothy Marshall Bowen	10
Autumn	Susan White	11
Christmas Party	James Ayrey	12
The Way To Live	Doris Huff	13
The Sermon On The Mount	Marlene Allen	14
Facts Are Facts	Alistair McLean	16
Wisdom	Winifred Parkinson	17
Bebe	John W Dossett-Davies	18
Old Burma	Ernest Jones	19
A Health Fanatic	F C Pelton	20
Jack	Diane Campbell	21
Loving Friends	Rosemary Sheridan	22
Rainbow Folk (A Plea)	Elwyn Johnson	23
Edna's Song	Irene Greenall	24
Broken Hearted	Karen Stephens	25
Dad I Want To Thank You	Stephen A Owen	26
Pay Homage	Corwin Barber	27
Though Not A Child, I Was Still Young When You Died . . .	Edi Little	28
The Rose Smiled	Elizabeth Stephens	29
Bluebells And Towers	James S Cameron	30
Unrequited (Jim And Babs) Love (1925)	Rosemary Peach	31
Angeline	Maureen J Hollands	32
Gold, Digging For Buried Treasure	John Burns	33

Is This Me?	Jim Pritchard	34
Sweet Spring At Rydal Mount	Ian L Fyfe	35
Why?	Harry Skinn	36
Useless Muses	I Mills	37
Europe 2000	Michael Murray	38
A Question Of Refugees	Allain St Clement	39
Marvels Of Creation : Birds	Reg James	40
Always On The Go	Anthony Higgins	41
My Family	Kathleen Wheeler	42
Before The Throne	John Harrold	44
The Owl	Jean Ford	45
Time And Space	Bryan Sammer	46
Arms Of Love	Malcolm Peter Mansfield	47
Preparation	Heather Moore	48
Grandchildren	Veronica Buckby	49
Accident Prone	Lachlan Taylor	50
Little Jesus	Judy Studd	51
The Visitors	John Pegg	52
The Actor	Dennis Studd	54
Scenario In A Restaurant	Terry Daley	55
Your Perception Of Perfection	Sue Southgate	56
I've Seen It All	Prince Rhan Of Kathari	58
Worker Griffiths	H G Griffiths	59
To Feel	Sam Dodman	60
To Aldeburgh Poetry Trust	John J Flint	61
September 11th 2002	James MacCreath	62
A Memorial To A Great Man	R T Owen	63
Seeking Peace	Ann Ormesher	64
In Flight	John Doyle	65
My Redeemer	Brenda Russell	66
The Penalty	James Hibbeler	67
Text Craze	Chandra	68
Brothers	Sue Knott	69
Sisters	Laura Perkins	70
Pepperland	Alan Pow	71
Weary World	Marguerita Johnstone	72
The Little Colleen	Christine Isaac	73
Memories Of Love	Pamela Baily	74

Autumn	Erika Rollinson	75
For Matty 'Pon Angel's Wing	Ron Matthews Jr	76
On Year On	George S Johnstone	77
Bosom Friend	Albert W Day	78
Dedicated To Poppy	Den Evans	79
A Tribute To Jackie	Flossie	80
The Tangled Web	Sheila Graham	81
My Love Forever	J Thompson	82
Lost Love	Nancy Reeves	83
Lilias Day	Tracy Patrick	84
An Ode To Margaret	David Livingstone	85
Now	Paul Wilkins	86
Huskies In The Snow	Angus Richmond	87
Benidorm's Not For Me	Val Stephenson	88
Dream Spirit	D G W Garde	90
Who Takes The Blame?	Nicola Esther Pearson	91
Yesterday	Edward L Smith & Carmen M Pursifull	92
Lost Friends . . .	Michael F Bullock	93

A Moment In Time

I remember being there; on the touchline;
All those years ago; as though on the threshold of life.
Enraptured by the passionate rugby, on the vibrating pitch,
In the twilight hush of Bath; that sultry September night.

I captured the moment in time; even then;
Suddenly aware of freedom, excitement, ecstasy.
The abandonment of home, childhood, discipline;
Replaced by something completely different.

I cannot recall the ensuing minutes, hours, days;
Just a precious, haunting memory remains;
As it always will; whilst the fervent years rush by;
Until the hushed time; in the twilight of my life.

Elizabeth Higgins

We're English

We're just as English, as English can be,
Who live in this island surrounded by sea,
See the dear flag, the flag of St George,
It makes those who hate us choke on their gorge.

Our love for our Queen who rules over this land,
The 'septics' all over just don't understand,
To those who say 'a republic we'd like',
Our answers to them is ~ 'go take a hike'.

These shores have been invaded as history shows,
By legions from Rome, who came here as foes,
The Vikings, the Normans, the Spanish as well,
Hitler didn't make it though he put us through hell.

We're integrated now, a true polyglot,
And welcome all those who will throw in their lot,
'Multi-culture' now is the word we must learn,
As hand-in-hand our country's living we earn.

The Government today is not up to much,
We'd have fared better under 'Screaming Lord Sutch',
So come back dear Sir Winston, we need your firm hand,
To restore, once again, pride in our land.

Pauline Brown

Chloroform Crescendo

Flicked tricked scatter
twitch to the shadow on
the beat.

Vann Scytere

The Snowman's Lament

'Tis chilly out here,' said the snowman,
'There's an icicle stuck on my nose,
My head has turned into an ice block
And I'm frozen right down to my toes.

I had a warm feeling inside me
When I was all pristine and new,
But now that I'm ragged and tattered
I'm discarded just like an old shoe.

I might be an awful lot warmer
If my hat with the wind hadn't gone,
I might be a little more cheery
If I'd hands to put some gloves on.

My scarf blew away in a blizzard
I miss it although it was old,
And now I've just started sneezing
I'm sure that I'm catching a cold.

I'm usually bright and so happy,
I'm not one to moan and complain
But the sky's getting darker each minute
And it looks like it's going to rain.

I've sung little songs to keep cheerful
But you have to admit it's not nice
To be stood there for hours in all weathers
When your body is made out of ice.

I really had thought you'd take pity
I'm sure it's not too much to ask,
Can I come and sit down by your fireside
And share some hot soup from your flask?

We'll snuggle up cosy together
And shut out the wild winter blast,
To wait for the first signs of springtime
When I can be warmer at last.

I may be so cold on the outside
But just in case you're in doubt
My heart is as warm as an ember
Please let me come in to thaw out.

'Tis chilly out here,' said the snowman,
Then along came a bright sunny day,
He must have felt warm in the sunshine
As he silently melted away.

Cherry Lea Lawton

Deep In Our Hearts

Deep in our hearts
we dance the greatest waltz,
commit the most devious crime,
laugh the loudest laugh,
and harbor the darkest secrets.

Deep in our hearts
we view the most hideous death
yet dream the happiest dream,
a dream that will carry
us onwards and forwards
to the brightest light of our
being enraptured with the
shiniest star, a star that will guide
us with our most troubled thoughts
lighting the pathway to
finding our beauteous dreams, and
answers to life's enigmas.
A poem for all eternity,
one that sings, a melody to carry us
tripping and laughing with our fondest
hopes and aspirations.

Deep in our hearts we dance the
greatest waltz.

Myra Selvadurai

Together

To find a place in someone else's space
When they've found their place in their space
Is not to trash it abuse it
but to . . .
Respect it, cherish it, honour it . . .
It's their space
They deserve the right to create their own space
It's clear
Discovering, learning melancholy, love, fear!
Remember!
It's still their space!
No matter how hard you look them in the face . . .
Oh please let me in and see
I'll bring you wonder, music, festivity
But what! will you bring me?
Will you invade my space and my privacy . . .
Or shall we simply melt into a wonderful
Intimacy . . .

Adele C W Lane

Heartache

'Did you hear what I said Irene?' the Doctor asked,
she never flinched, he was astonished at the way she sat,
he thought she'd misheard. 'Yes Doctor, I've got cancer,
my life is now in your hands,' was the answer.
So positive she would return home, she fulfilled
little obligations. (Her uprighteousness).
After a preliminary examination the operation followed.
Which was a success, her progress was good, when we left her,
she was joking with the patients. Next day a phone call.
'Come quickly, she's deteriorating.' When we arrived she had
passed away (Pulmonary Thromboembolism).

Then I thought I heard Angels singing,
to music sweet and low
for God had taken our Irene.
Suddenly!
We didn't want her to go.
She climbed that marble staircase
to those renowned Pearly Gates.
God bade His Angels,
'Open them wide, for her I've reserved a place.'
With outstretched arms she was welcomed
To God's Gift ~ her Heavenly Home.
Then onward she walked alongside them
to meet loved ones she'd known.

Those left on Earth are heartbroken.
Seemingly looking like shells.
We hope each morn we awaken
'Twas only a dream ~ and all's well.
It's painful losing a loved one,
the good things they've done sorely missed.
If only ~ she could stand beside us
then by all of us ~ hugged and kissed.

    Peggy Johnson

Dreams Part 3
(Dedicated to Sue Nicholson)

Where are you dream girl
Won't you come to me
and be my bride?
It kills me not having you
when you should be mine.

I need your tender touch
and I need your sweet kisses,
I can't wait for you to appear
in front of my eyes,
hold me until the break of dawn.

Where do you go
when the sun comes up?
Can't you stay a little longer
in these arms of mine?
Won't you stay with me?

You're there when I fall asleep
but you're gone when I wake,
hold my hand tight
until we leave the night
and enter the daytime.

Chris T Barber

The World At Peace

2002 how far have we come
The first and second world war,
It's go fight the Hun
In my lifetime
There was always a war ~ some place,
For here to a far distant shore.
Never no end to trouble and strife
Why, was we all given ~ this life?
Human conflict, wars never end,
Planning and talking, peacemakers we send.
They say it's survival, the fittest and all,
What a world of trouble
Why should be bother, at all!
But we do all the time
And we try to move on,
This world we live in, it just goes on.
We have to have faith and peace in our hearts,
And just perhaps one day
The world, will have a heart ~
That's together, with peace for all
How wonderful life would be,
At least it would be a start.
No more heartache, fighting, and hate,
Would be good to see all cultures
Sitting together, at their place,
Talking of peace, love and not war,
A future for the children, as never before.
The past, we leave behind
Make a brave new world
With enough in the world, to feed all.
No famine, or sickness, a place to belong
Helping each other, all to be strong.
To plan for a future, that's simple and good
Wouldn't it be wonderful
If only we could ~

   Dorothy Marshall Bowen

Autumn

We'll drink to the traditional gang
and take a grape to Tout la Monde.
Like a squirrel that stores its nuts
is a must for when he returns is
hoping for heaven maybe a lucky seven.

The golden leaves will hide the weeds
The witches spell to make it sell
Or do something, free scones for tea
for you and me, maybe some apple pie
if you help a passer-by.

To steal not much of a meal, still you can keel
Wash your hands, strike up the big band
and keep away from places like Dresden and the blitz
away from peoples who like their kicks.

Susan White

Christmas Party

I'm inviting you home for Christmas.
Because I'm on my own.
We can have a party,
I'll arrange it all by phone.
I'll invite my friends and neighbours,
We'll all have a real swell time.
I don't know who will pay for it,
Because I haven't got a dime.
We can all get rather merry,
I'll even invite a band.
I'm sure because it's Christmas
That they will understand.
I can't pay for the party
But everything's underhand.
When the party's over
And the people disappear
I'll invite everyone for Christmas,
But it'll have to be next year.

James Ayrey

The Way To Live

Live life to the full whatever your age
You are your own person the world is your stage
You slip into the world a person to make a place
To live your life with enough space
To create your own background
Your life is a challenge meet it head high
Don't lose heart if trouble seems nigh
Pause
Look around
Find some firm ground
With renewed hope you'll cope with setbacks
You'll gather strength then go to any length to beat them
Go forward with a smile as you travel each mile.

Doris Huff

The Sermon On The Mount

Jesus took his followers up a mountain high
Far from the noisy clamour of the town,
And there they sat and listened, enthralled by
His uplifting 'Sermon on the Mount'.

He told them that the poor in spirit are blessed;
To them belongs the Kingdom of Heaven.
He said also that the merciful are blest
And to them shall mercy be given.

He said blessed are the people that mourn;
God's comfort to them will be given,
Happy knowing that the day will surely dawn
When all that grieve are united in Heaven.

He said God blesses those that are meek,
Those who count themselves of little worth,
Who no high position or grandeur seek;
They alone shall inherit the earth.

Those who hunger and thirst for what is right
Are blessed; their hunger shall be fed.
The pure in heart too are blessed aright;
Their reward, they shall see our God.

He told them too the peacemakers are blessed,
Who challenge tyranny and the iron rod.
They shall be known as, and addressed
As, how enviable, children of God.

Blest are those who suffer for God's sake,
Accepting insults and hostile stares,
Who all manner of calumny happily take;
The Kingdom of Heaven is theirs.

How comforting those words must have been
To His followers as they went on their way,
And the message of hope contained therein
Is just as true to this very day.

    Marlene Allen

Facts are Facts

When in sufferance's name of amity
    A stop put to this peoples' enmity?
To walk the streets to sleep in your bed,
    Who is it in the name is being led
Down tunnels desperate that all are bled?
    Is it fear, misguided wisdom,
Instructions from another planet dealt them,
    That they no sight of a slightest trickle
Of fertile membranes not so fickle?
    Pick up the threads all hence askance
And table us that one last chance
    To walk the streets and sleep in our beds;
To think to defend and to enhance,
    The ways to go, and not retreat
To those who lie inept in the streets.
    The day will come when out of tether,
Folk will say the time is nigh,
    To grant jurisdiction, long overdue,
To hide away those no longer able
    And treat the ones who abide the stable
Of gain, of greed, and turn the table;
    To see the faces squirm whereon
The hangman's noose it does a-beckon;
    To see the march, retreat en-masse
The jellies now who were brave syne,
    Who'll be just angels, for all their time.

Alistair McLean

Wisdom

Wisdom only comes, when you have lived a life
I now could write a book on love and crime.
Because you see, I've been given time
Suffering is only a part of it, tears are very special
We cry for ourselves ~ so we must work to improve.
Life is never easy, it's hard and difficult
Just one day at a time.
Expect no mercy from man, woman, or child.
Clean and polish now, no matter how little then is.
Sweat, strain, push and tame, keep smiling if you dare.
Give cuddles, give food, give yourself.
All will soon be returned
Then wisdom reaches out, and takes you by the hand
Leading you to light
A bright and stunning light.
No one can ever hurt you again
As all pleasures are now yours.
Wisdom gains all things
So be wise now, reach out and try, and hold tight.

Winfred Parkinson

Bebe

Bebe
Dark Lady of the Night
And of the summer too

Of childhood days
You remind me
With your oval face and dark hair

Your smooth skin
And your Cheshire accent
How do you torment me so

Is your spell
Security
In an insecure world
Is it a promise
Of what life could be

Is it an echo
From long ago
Of being tucked
Into bed
And kissed goodnight

Dark Lady of the Night
And of the summer too
Why do you torment me so

John W Dossett-Davies

Old Burma

A market place in Mandalay
With fragrant spices on display
The Gold Pagodas in the sun
And firing of a noonday gun.

Some Burma girls with Raven hair
and temple Bells that call to Prayer
the silent Buddha's mystic stare.
With Rickshaws weaving here and there

and in the clamour and the throng
the Shaven headed Monks in Song
to Watch the sun from China Rise
the Jungles and the burning Plains
and then incessant Monsoon Rains.

Ernest Jones

A Health Fanatic

I'm a health fanatic,
The measures I take to keep healthy,
Are drastic and dramatic.
I spend a lot of time in the gym,
They say it's good for me,
But it gives me a painful grin.
I use all the lotions,
And I swallow all the pills,
To keep myself super fit,
And not have any nasty ills.
I take so many tablets,
When I walk I rattle.
To keep the nasty bugs away,
It is a constant battle.
Some people think I'm paranoid,
Any possible source of infection
I deliberately avoid.
All the ways the bugs can get me,
I have now completely shut.
I've become a hermit,
And am living in a hut.

F C Pelton

Jack

Big, black Jack,
Better known as Elias Gold,
So gentle of nature,
A heart so bold,
His short five years have seen him become,
A right good greyhound, who could really run,
He was placed and won many races,
Now a life with me, he faces,
A soft warm bed, food and care,
Of me and the future, he has no scare,
He was so shy and so unsure,
His shell he has left, his trust so pure,
He really is a lovely lad,
He knows how to be good, not bad,
And when he comes to me of his own free will,
Tail wagging, eyes bright, ready for love,
I see a little star, fallen from the night sky, from far up above.

Diane Campbell

Loving Friends

There's a corner, in my heart
It's special for friends
I've been blessed
Along my way
Giving courage, that I've lacked
Inspiration, certainly needed that
Friendly people sharing themselves
How happy can life be
Knowing never far from me
Truly very comforting
Their fragrance as a rose
Lovely friends known
Much appreciate
My precious moments
Corner in my heart fulfilled
Bubbles over remembering memories.

Rosemary Sheridan

Rainbow Folk (A Plea)

Why did you born us many coloured,
A variant in every creed?
How can we cry Hallelujah!
When we know not of your need,
White or Brown, Yellow tinged or Black,
We are but rainbows of earth's scheme,
Why then can we not blend harmoniously,
As does the aftermath arc supreme?
In the solitude of the quiet moment,
When the mind is hallowed in grace,
Are the listening Gods' to the prayer talk several,
Or channel tunnelled, with but one station place?
Do we, as each one and every,
Seek to turn our face to apply,
Or do we don familiarities habit,
Of a journey man who merely says 'aye'?
Since time first begin its sentence,
In the uncertainty of our minds,
We have offered up our soliloquies,
To the many Icons of diverse kinds.
Always the searching, always the striving,
To the vindication of our soul.
The embodiment which within us seeks,
A nirvana as our goal.
O why can't those who depart before us,
Be a mere shoulder glance assigned,
A whisper aside with which to confide,
To the one due to follow behind?
Resolve for us then this problem,
Remove us from this segregating yoke.
So henceforth and always thereafter,
We can truly be called Rainbow Folk.

Elwyn Johnson

Edna's Song
*(Dedicated to my dear friend, Edna Dolman,
who died on 1st January 2001)*

Dear Lord, take Edna's soul and accept it
    gently into your hands,
It is wrapped around with love and service
    to others, with golden bands,
She will have stars of love in her eyes
    and diamonds glistening in her hair,
They will be shining and radiate brightness,
    and her face will be oh! so fair.

She will join the choir of heavenly angels lauding your
    praises in beautiful song,
Still helping others on life's highway and yet,
    to you, she will belong,
She will do her work in heaven as she did
    on this lowly earth,
God bless you, dear Edna, we will remember
    you, and know your true worth.

Irene Greenall

Broken Hearted

I offer to you, my broken heart,
Open it up and make a new start.
Come walking with me hand in hand,
Together on everything, let us stand.
Let the love inside us grow,
Then in our day to day lives, let it show.
Make me really happy once more,
Only you then will I ever adore.
Kiss me, hold me, don't let go,
Let me true love come to know.
Stay with me, let us never part,
I'll let only you into my heart.
Allow our emotions to freely flow,
Silence my upset and my every woe.
Talk to me and ease my troubled mind,
Let me see you're loving, warm and kind.
My tender heart is waiting for you,
To share a love that's sincere and true.

Karen Stephens

Dad I Want To Thank You

I grew up in a tough world,
But in my Dad's world
He taught me to be strong.
Be kind to people.
Be sure to listen well.
And try your best to love everyone.

My Dad has always been there for me,
I've put him at the top of my family tree
As a boy I was only interested in playing with my toys.
Playing football after school.
Breaking all of my parents' rules.
I didn't have much time to spend with my Dad.
Not that I didn't care.
I was far too busy being a kid somewhere.

I remember waiting at the gate
For him to return after work
He'd always have a treat for me.
Being the youngest of five,
Guess it was my little perk.
And he'd spend hours teaching me to play the guitar.
I didn't have much time for a remote controlled care.

All my life I don't think I have told him,
Just how much he means to me.
'Cos it's something us men find hard to do.
It doesn't come easily
Saying how much I love you.
I think my Dad's great.
More than that he's also my mate.

Now I'm a man myself Dad.
All I have I owe it all to you.
And now I have my own world.
Dad I want to thank you.

    Stephen A Owen

Pay Homage

Pay homage to me
O mere mortals
for I am the omniscient one.

The one of ages,
the one of all times.

I have seen you bow yourselves
down before false gods,
for they are not gods
but fools.

Whoever it is you follow
be it, the so called god,
Satan, Allah, Siva or Brahma;
for it is written in the book of darkness,
that they shall all be struck down
with the power of a thousand thunderstorms
and so will all their followers.

    Corwin Barber

though not a child, i was still young when you died . . .

though not a child
i was still young when you died
the memories short formed
hand held and shaky

i'm never quite sure
just how well i knew you
what i always remember
is how much i want to

mother to my mother
known as mary to others
you were born of the land
i love and call home

few photos record
someone older than you
someone quiet, someone still
someone colder than you

i've never gone looking
nor once have i asked
to ink in the details
of my kirlian glass

but here in these fields
behind the church of your absence
i replace the wonder with warmth
reunited at last

edi little

The Rose Smiled

The rose smiled at the sun in dazzling dream,
And the pulsing heart of the rose was cream.

To morning dew did daisy petals unfold
And the pulsing heart of the daisy was gold.

Moonlight peered at man through a window crack
And the pulsing heart of the man was black.

Elizabeth Stephens

Bluebells And Towers

Compensating and arranging,
Love's guiding hand,
Like a miracle of light upon the land,
Following the brightest Angel across the sand.

Producing coloure'd rainbows inspiring,
Where silver and gold stars formulate,
Acknowledging God's brilliant power,
Creatively drawn and executed beside the heavenly tower.

There through a secret garden is the marble summerhouse,
Where wild ivy creeps on fore'er more.
The white mist hangs in plates,
Next to the giant golden gates.

Peace and quietness prevails,
Sequestered and remote,
In bliss and solitude,
Thinking and dreaming of my lover.

Where wild birds and bees sing harmoniously,
The four seasons change continuously,
There growing are beautiful flowers,
Now seeing a wondrous carpet of bluebells and towers.

Like a fairy tale castle with the shadow of the moon,
With watery moats and gardens of bloom.
Where a thousand white horses fly,
Singing happily are Fairies and gnomes.

Making a thousand and one wishes,
By the glittering waterfall dive silver and gold fishes.
Where giant bubbles float, scattering afar,
Oh how I wonder at its pleasantries.

James S Cameron

Unrequited (Jim And Babs) Love (1925)

She wrote him a 'Dear John' letter
As she said it would be better
Not to see one another no more
As, he seemed to think of his mother
Much, much, more than her. No holiday either!
As on Saturday nights, he kept her waiting
A full thirty minutes, anticipating an
Evening of laughter and love, but
His mother would not let him go
Which made an evening, full of woe.
Better to find out now, that
I don't care for you, like I used to.
That amount of money I cannot save
So cancel my rooms, and call it a day.
Take Mum with you, and forget me
No way can we be together, that I can see.
Your Mum comes first, in all that you do
That is something I could rue.
To return my presents, please tell Sid
I will give them to him, if it's what you wish
Remember me, to Mum, Lil and Flo, explain
That I have to go, elsewhere, and I hope
That you will find happiness, and in time
Forget me! Do not try to stop me, I will
Not change my mind, Helen has no need to write
For love is blind, don't try to see me, as I am
Out to you, thanks for the good time, but
This day we will rue!

Rosemary Peach

Angeline
(Dedicated to my Grandsons Kyle aged 4, and Oliver aged 1)

Angeline, is a small lady bug, she has 25 children so there's plenty to hug.
They dwell in a mattress all cosy and snug, next to very nice neighbours who live in a rug.

It's a very large mattress so there's plenty to spare, and there's always a corner for some bug to share.
Her sister she lives in the bedroom next door, she has several children and she's expecting some more.
Her brother he dwells in a rug on the floor, and their cousin abides in the bed by the door.

They all live in a doll's house that is dusty and old, high up in an attic that is terribly cold.
The attic belongs to an old ruined house, nobody lives there, not even a mouse.
Apart from the occupants mentioned above, so cosy and snug as a bug-in-a-rug.

Maureen J Hollands

Gold, Digging For Buried Treasure

Gold, digging for buried treasure
finds it. Snatches.
The treasure refuses to budge.
Once discovered there is no escape.
Tugs, heaves, drops it.
One foot clamps the writhing thing.
From beak to claw
stretches it like a jelly baby,
till twang ~ red curls around gold.
He begins to absorb his catch,
all the while watching,
watching me.
A moment still, senses focused,
staring me out.
Would I try to chase him away
to gain the prize for myself?
Such a prize. Perhaps a bigger prize?
Decides I am no threat.
Meal over, this blackbird
just hops away
to the edge of my garden,
a corner of his kingdom,
safe in the knowledge of two victories.

John Burns

Is This Me?

'I can't stand the modern kids they are always making noise,
it's hard to tell which sort they are they could be girls or boys,
they cycle on the pavements and up a one way street ~
I can't remember the last time that one offered me a seat.'

'Hang on a minute Granny who was that at your front door?
I'm sure it was young Kate and Fred who live at number four,
they come in every morning to see that you're alright ~
then race away to school each day, then call most every night.'

'They often do your shopping, draw the curtains or make tea ~
and though I don't call every day they will always phone me,
you know you like the family especially Kate and Fred,
I wish that you saw other things not just what makes you see red.'

'That is all the TV tells me ~ bad news is all I read,
there just seems nothing good out there just violence and greed,
I sit and read ~ and hear it all, *and young folk cause mayhem*
I don't *know* many Young Folk
but I know all of them.'

Jim Pritchard

Sweet Spring At Rydal Mount

Ah! Sweet spring at Rydal Mount!
with daffodils in radiant bloom,
Soon the trees will bear their foliage,
Oh! Such a cry from winter gloom.
Along the stony path I walk
through God's Garden in solitude,
I gaze at the hills surrounding me,
majestic, rugged ~ sets the mood.
The welcome wing of the befriending bird
that follows me around,
This place so tranquil ~ so embracing,
such magnificent beauty to astound.
Ah! Lakeland with your snow-capped peaks
and purifying air,
With gurgling streams and Rydal Water
and Loughrigg Fell ~ so debonair.
Once Wordsworth walked along this way
in byegone yesteryear,
I can almost feel his presence now,
allaying any fear.
Perhaps I feel his inspiration
as in his footsteps I walk along,
Through wooded glades and sunlit beauty,
with a chorus of birds in morning song.
Ah! Sweet Spring at Rydal Mount!
with daffodils abound,
to join in thanks at Rydal Church,
with joyful voice I now resound!

Ian L Fyfe

Why?

Why oh why can't we live in peace
Muslims and Christians if you please
Why oh why do we have to die
Just because of a man with an evil eye

The men who took control of those planes
Killing thousands must have been insane
Flying the planes into the World Trade Towers
Killing the helpless passengers in their power

Why are some men filled with an evil dement
To destroy civilization is their one intent
Terrorists have no feeling for the rest of mankind
Greed, power and killing is all they have in mind

But why oh why do we have to fight
It would be wonderful if we could put the world right
Christians and Muslims living in peace
All nations should try for all wars to cease

We could all walk around with a smile on our face
It would be a dream come true for every race
So why can't all mankind live in harmony today
What joy and happiness to live this heavenly way

Harry Skinn

Useless Muses

I found a needle wi'out an eye,
I just couldn't thread it,
I readily did try,
I found a sparkling silver button,
It hadn't a hole,
I couldn't sew it on,
I found a buckle wi'out a belt,
I tried to tie it up with string,
'Twas wasted effort, I felt,
I found a man wi'out his dog,
Lost he was and alone,
Just like my needle wi'out an eye,
A kettle wi'out a stone,
I found a lark wi'out a song,
A whistle wi'out a blow,
Now that's not right, something's gone wrong,
A river wi'out its flow,
I found a leaf wi'out its tree,
All red it was and brown,
And all its edges were curled up,
To take the winter to town,
I found a cat wi'out a mouse,
A dog wi'out a cat,
A monkey wi'out a trace of a louse,
A church wi'out a bat,
I found a cross wi'out a Christ,
A mundane sight to see,
But worst of all these peculiar things,
A Yew wi'out a me.

I Mills

Europe 2000

Crunching boot on stone and slate
awaken the sentry at the menin gate,
a father cries 'for god sake wait,'
but lights are dim and the day is late.

Splashing blood on the door and sill
nothing changes nothing will,
a mother pleads, 'be still'! 'be still'!
when lights are dim the soldiers kill.

Rumbling tank from another state
rubbled street and village fete,
ask the children why they hate,
when lights are dim and the day is late.

Father, mother, daughter, son,
see them tremble as they run
out of history's blackened gate
once again from smoking gun,
once again from fife and drum,
and marching feet on ancient slate.

Michael Murray

A Question Of Refugees

How do we identify a refugee, is there a basic conception?
It is *always* someone on the move fleeing from possible detention?
When denied everything but life itself, living without just cause,
Who should we blame when they're put to flight from regimes that disregard laws?
Do we picture a person dressed in rags with a lifetime's achievements carried in bags?
Or a man in a suit that he's slept in or women resembling old hags.
Is the refugee's dream always the same, with peace and freedom a constant aim?
Nowhere to sleep and no food to eat, is it wonder they admit to defeat?
From what does their frustration come? Repression and poverty, but only for some.
Think of suppression and freedom of speech and the political constraints in place.
For such is the life of the pre-refugee, do they ever have much to praise?
Do the pictures that appear promote urgency to deal with asylum seekers?
Not yet we are told by those who are bold, *you* know, the ones who're the speakers.
Are we at liberty to draw comparisons? When we eat and sleep at will, and are able to dispel life's ailments by merely taking a pill.
We've not yet talked about colour but you'd find that it does have a bearing.
It's no guess that the whiter your skin is you'll find plenty of folks that are caring.
The division of wealth would seem to be, inadequate and totally unfair, but it's doubtful is many would lightly agree to give up a small part of their share.
Liberty, Fraternity and Egalité are meaningful and sound, but sounds die away unrecognised leaving nothing. It's all too profound.

Allain St Clement

Marvels Of Creations : Birds

From my ivied lattice window
I see the twittering birds at play
And captured by their antics
I watch them come and go all day
And every now and then perch on my sill
To feed on titbits as they take their fill.

These creatures cherished long by man
Be it the robin, lark or wren
Or blackbird, sparrow, bluetit, owl,
Near towns or on the open fen,
And some are coloured, some are brown and dun,
But Birds of Paradise thrive in the sun.

What of the wingèd angel-host?
Did man conjecture wings for these?
In ancient times their paintings show
On icons, statues, tapestries,
All through the ages they have played their part
To yearning mankind and uplift the heart.

Reg James

Always On The Go

One can always depend
On our happy friend
Sending a card
Nothing is too hard
Racing round in a fit
To get that bit
Whatever, one needs
Cotton or beads
Eating Sunday roast
Will fly to coast
If heavy load
Will hit the road
There is no doubt
In her runabout
Walking at a pace
Our girl's having a race
Shift and shout
She's got clout
Having fun
Always on the run
Things to show
Our Sylvia, always on the go

    Anthony HIggins

My Family

Dad was quite a handsome man
But he didn't have the knack:
Instead of working eight till five,
He went round with a pack.

Mother was hard working
Making clothes and mending shoes,
Her beautiful washing on the line
Gave envious folk the blues.

Douglas knows a thing or two
Is a wizard at turning wood,
Gardening and making wine,
And wrote a book that's good.

Winnie with her many skills
Gives a lot of people pleasure.
She works hard helping others,
Not much time for leisure.

Elsie and her lacemaking
No one can surpass.
If you want to do it right
You'd better join her class.

Vera's nimble fingers
Make lots of pretty things.
The joy we share together,
My heart truly sings.

Repairing cars he's no mug,
At Bernard take a look.
Woodwork and gardening,
He can also cook.

I'm not very clever,
But I think a lot.
I will tell you one thing,
I'm glad for what I've got

Kathleen Wheeler

Before The Throne

When I stand before His throne,
clothed in beauty not my own.
What will He say to me?
'Just enter in,
come on home.'

As I stand there all amazed
seeing with my eyes all glazed,
His beauty and His grace.
Heavenly place,
now my home.

No thoughts concerning my past,
my sinful life has gone at last.
Life is so new for me,
now I can see
that I'm home.

John Harrold

The Owl

The earth is warm, the moon shines bright
The owl hoots upon the wing
In the still of the night
Standing on chimney pots so tall
Surveying the land around once more
What does he see he can but tell
A mouse, a mole, a fox's tail.
There he dives swift and silent
Now his prey lies dormant
Life in the night is much the same
As cloud sunshine and rain
God's gift to earth is given back
To Him above in Heaven.

 Amen

 Jean Ford

Time And Space

Dark is the night, there is no light,
Save that from the moon and myriad stars:
In that dark void, without any walls,
Hang planets, Venus, Jupiter and Mars.

Along the Milky Way, it's said,
Are many wond'rous sights,
There the malevolent Black Hole lurks,
Moving, spinning, into a planet it bites.

Swirling, twisting galaxies are there,
And mystical comets can be found,
Formed in a bygone age, far out,
Orbiting our Sun, held gravity bound.

Moon and stars twinkle and shine,
But what is out there, out of sight:
Things beyond our wildest dreams,
Hiding in that perpetual night?

Bryan Sammer

Arms Of Love

He liked her straight from the start
She had scaled the fortress walls
And without arrow or malice . . .
Pierced his silent
But still vibrant . . . heart.

No film for the camera
No script written;
Though even so . . .
Like some Hollywood screenplay
The situation unacted
Did roll.

The yearly staff dance
A chance for romance
Or sadly . . .
Perhaps . . .
No second glance.

She was there alone
Her boyfriend
Working the twilight zone.
Happy with friends
She danced till the music ended.
Until some nameless individual
Uninvited on her private world descended.

But then noble as he was
And her boyfriend's friend also . . .
Or maybe just because.

He simply
In saviour mode
Her honour defended.

Malcolm Peter Mansfield

Preparation

I've cut the hedges and trimmed the edges
Mowed the lawn, till completely shorn
It's hard to believe I've been up since dawn
Must clean the tools and sort the seeds
In preparation for the war on weeds
I've pruned and sprayed ~ phew, what a day!
Done all this and get no pay
My friends all said, 'When you retire ~ you'll
    put your feet up by the fire'
So, after I've cleared the path I'm going to take a Radox bath
    and look back on the day and have a b----y laugh.

Heather Moore

Grandchildren

Today I've had a lovely day
I've been a 'good girl' my daddy did say
My mummy you know, has lots to do
I love her lots and my sister too

Soon I will be having my tea
And playing a little ~ with toys maybe
Bathtime next, before I go to bed
And say goodnight when I rest my head

In just a minute I'm going to sleep
Before I do I'll just take a peep
Out of my window ~ up in the sky
The stars and moon so very high

I close my eyes and start to dream
Of what a lovely day it has been
I hope tomorrow will be as good
If I wish very hard, perhaps it could.

Goodnight God bless to everyone
Thank you Jesus for all I've done
'Chloe's' my name and I love you
For making me happy each day through.

Veronica Buckby

Accident Prone

My life has been a wilderness
    though I put my faith in God
I have been highly traumatized
    that I believe he is a fraud

I have been punished so unkindly
    yet I do not think I sin
But I cannot find the answer here
    to know where to begin

I have cried myself to sleep at night
    and dread the coming of the morn
With the cruel knocks I've had
    I wish I'd not been born

With each accident I try to bear
    the pain that always follows
But often there is another comes
    which makes it hard to swallow

But still I try to carry on
    in the hope my God one day
Will make things much more cheerful
    so I can enjoy the Christian way.

Lachlan Taylor

Little Jesus
(Away with the manger)

Dragged from a cardboard box
I am all arranged so neatly
Set up on display
I smile at them so sweetly.

I cannot be a threat
whilst I am in a stable
A baby cannot talk you see
because I am not able.

They take me out at Christmas
and put me in a manger
Then safely have a look
where I can be no danger.

I really am so hurt
for one day I'll be a man
No longer in a baby's crib
no more a Peter Pan

For when this season's over
and festive cheer is through
then, soon it will be Easter
and then what will they do?

Judy Studd

The Visitors

These visitors that come,
They leave a distortion, a ripple in the air.
I feel a touch on my shoulder, turn around,
But of course there's no one there.
Cats and people I glimpse at the corner of my eye,
Turning is a little unnerving,
But how easy is it for my eyes to lie?
Sometimes a sweet scent pervades the room,
Drifting like a summer garden's warm perfume.
The old folks say Heaven's Summerland lies open,
Someone close to me will be passing over soon.
At times some far away melody plays for me,
A long forgotten tune.
Or I hear people quietly talking,
Which ceases as I enter the room.
Not a living soul is there of course,
Just a chamber deep in gloom.
Why do they need to visit me this way?
It should fill me with some dismay,
But in truth I'd be more interested what they have to say.
But they always seem so keen to get away.
These fleeting shades and shadows,
Drift like clouds across the moon,
Vaporous; they disperse all too soon,
But what's this I've found,
A small white feather lying on the ground?
Can this be a celestial calling card?
But might this be a mistake,
Could not a feather have fallen,
When I shook the duck-down pillowcase?

Reason or make-believe lies open to me,
But on this midwinter Yuletide night,
I'll ignore the mundane,
And settle for a Christmas fantasy.
It's not very hard, a metre's so close to a yard,
To believe it's my guardian angel's calling card.

John Pegg

The Actor
(All the world's a stage and every man and woman merely players ~ William Shakespeare)

The actor stood silent in the spotlight as it arced its way across the auditorium, and began to consider the next part he had to play. Knowing that he could no longer return to the past, he began to feel the fresh breath of this new part as it began to struggle within him, searching for a way out; seeking fulfilment in itself.
Briefly, he began to consider the many parts he had played.
'What had he been?' he mused. The sinner, the convert, the father, the judge ... glimpses of his life passed before him, each a part of his being; each having had its own part to play in moulding his life until he reached the place where he now stood.

A great kaleidoscope of dreams, untold stories, great scenes enacted against a backdrop of time, all flashed through his mind in these last moments of preparation.

Watching him stand there, preparing his lines, trying out his new voice, I began to wonder how he would feel as the curtains rose on the hardest part he would ever have to play ...

himself ...

Dennis Studd

Scenario In A Restaurant

I lingered over a leisurely lunch
In a rosy restaurant,
Gazing idly around 'til I noticed
A young couple intent,
In a corner, opposite each other.
I watched the scenario there.
At first the woman smiled so sweetly,
Then whispered to her partner.
The body language revealed the story
She held his hands close to.
I could not help overhearing her words,
'The children are missing you,
Please come home, we love you and want you back.'
The man only shook his head.
I could see her continuing to plead with him,
He continued shaking his head.
She seemed to lose her patience, her voice rose.
'You are selfish, mother warned me ~'
'Here comes the old story again,' said he.
'Why did I bother?' said she.
She stood up, then hurled her cup and contents,
And all over him it went.
He never reacted, just stood up
And walked out of the restaurant.

Terry Daley

Your Perception Of Perfection

I can never be what you want
Your idyll is too great ~
Beyond my ability or my desire.
I have faults ~
Some you are prepared to live with.
Others, you want to erase.

You have placed me on a pedestal.
From which I am destined to fall.
You want to gaze
On your perception of perfection.
But that's not the real me.

I am not perfect,
Nor will I ever be.
But I have much to give
To those who want to receive.
So, if you truly love me,
You'll love all that I am.
Not just the image of your love.
But the reality that stands before you.

I am like a glazed antique ~ made up of flaws and faults.
Yet full of character and charm.
A thing of beauty that is cherished
Despite its cracks and blemishes.
If you search beneath my damaged exterior
As if I too was such a prize,
Only then will you learn my true value.

If, having gazed upon this treasure ~
No longer in mint condition
But rather, now scarred and crazed
With character and mystery.
If then, it is still what you truly desire,
Accept it for what it is ~
Only then can you be
At one with that which you hold so dear.

Sue Southgate

I've Seen It All
(In dedication to Sylvia, my wife, my life)

Absolute bliss when I fell in love
Blessed by our dear Lord above
A beautiful girl and so divine
Knowing in time she would be mine

A wonderful feeling of joy and bliss
Always sealed with a loving kiss
A love that just grew and grew
To both of us our love was true

Then marriage, nothing but happiness all the time
Such love and joy is divine
Years and years, and oh such love
Still blessed by our Lord above

Suddenly my wife suffered a stroke
I was such a devastated bloke
So useless, there was nothing I could do
I felt as if my life was through

I became a slave to her every whim
Her thread of life now so slim
I refused to give up, I was after all still in love
But I questioned *why?* from our Lord above

Death stole her away whilst she slept
And a million tears I wept
But life must go on so they say
But now I was no longer happy and gay

I've so many happy memories and my wife's not dead
She lives on in my heart and head
Although many years have passed me by
I still find time to weep and cry

I've got treasured memories by the score
With my Christian faith I could not have had more

Prince Rhan of Kathari

Worker Griffiths

Worker Griffiths works in Wigston
For only £15 per week
Sees a box closed up
Picks it up and opens
The lid upon the box
A man inside does say
To put his hand inside
Worker Griffiths does just that
There follows a big flash
He finds himself in 2111
Where all are paid equally
He then makes a wish
That back in Century 21
Everyone gets paid the same
There follows another bright flash
And back in October 2001
Instead of a £15 pay packet
He receives £4.10 per hour
That's £102.50 per week

H G Griffiths

To Feel

It's one o'clock in the morning
    I feel enchanted by the moon up high
    I lean bare flesh on cold glass
    I gaze into the sky.

I can see my own reflection
    I stare beyond and deep
    I so enjoy this feeling
    It's one I long to keep.

Someone chose you to help me
    Look at what I just can't see
    Selected by fate or destiny
    To spark the fire in me.

So feel the emotion
    For I know that it could cease
    Please last forever
    I love you inner peace.

Sam Dodman

To Aldeburgh Poetry Trust

Too old for 'workshop' work-houses gone
Or to write a fifteenth century plain song
But is it not two thousand/'Goldings Lane'
Pain 'Golden Coach' no need try explain
Price paid for this Country many with life
Lottery with computer competition is rife
'Say money come easy' go's the same
Poor Albert the lion no one really blame

'Sample Poems; what after twelfth year
Or beer, planners money for nothing fear
Trust corruption to take much bigger bite
When not know difference 'left and right'

Outstanding like others, impetus inspiration
Do none of you care about British Nation
The gloom in our country if no kick a ball
Or ban MP, some ministers fly so tall
But the money who do it really come off
Now all British citizens a cold so much cough
Scoff at no law like some writers no bore
While those running country another tour

John J Flint

September 11th 2002

Back from school
The TV turns on,
To my horror
The Twin Towers are gone.
The north and south tower
Engulfed in flames,
People are screaming
But who is to blame?
People jumping
To their death
This was a day to remember
It was September 11th.
The news kept repeating
The planes' collision
The terrorists had hit the heart of America
With some precision.
The ground started to rumble
As the south tower collapsed,
The cloud of dust suffocated New York
But the devastation has not passed.
People ran away
As the north tower fell
Thousands of people dead,
This is everyone's hell.
The World Trade Center is gone
I feel there is no heaven.
This is a day of mourning
This is September 11th.

James McCreath (14)

A Memorial To A Great Man

My heart goes out to the family of the late Bill Owen
A well-loved actor of The Last of the Summer Wine
I have enjoyed every episode, which I have seen
Hair-raising stunts he went through as Compo, can be yours
                                                        and mine
Memories of this great little man, with a very big heart
He stood tall above the rest, even in his Wellington boots
With his two chums of this Trio, Oh! How he played his part
His mirth as a star in films and TV he will go with the great ones
I'm sure that the characters in the half hour on good clean fun
Will be sadly missed, he was the source of fun in their midst
After all the pranks show in this after its 26th year long run
Another 26 years would not go amiss; it must not be lost in times
                                                        of mists
These few lines are to show respect for the life of Bill Owen
I have written these words in a rather poetic way
All, who mourn over the gallant Bill Owen, with heads bowing
The tears of grief over his passing on, will we play straight and
                                                        not stray
He shared his fun with millions of the TV screen
Not to mention the wonderful support of his Co-Stars
As this memorable memory of a great and fine Human being
The character of 'Compo' is impossible to compare

    R T Owen

Seeking Peace

Too many tears in the world today
Are shed for the want of love.
Empty tomorrows become our challenge
Long forgotten joys on blank faces.

Children pick up on our despair
Believing their world is better.
We open their eyes and teach them our lies
Words, evil bearers of hurt and shame.

Too many sighs in the air we breathe,
Are shattered by the wings of a dove,
Our dreams become living nightmares
As we pretend this is what we want.

How can we put this right, our need
For love is greater than hate.
But nothing in life, our reality now
Will give us the peace that we seek.

Ann Ormesher

In Flight

Four swans skim the sea surface
Turning around the cove, across the bay
Flying straight into the setting sun
A sword of light
On this still day

They circle overhead
Booming out their flight plan
Leaving behind a lone observer
Transfixed by their departure.

John Doyle

My Redeemer

I know my redeemer lives.
He reigns on high.
His hand guides me.

So many times I feel His spirit
show me the way forward.
I stumble. I fall.

He lifts me up high again.
He clears the way.
Removes the obstacles
from my path.

He cuts them down with
His almighty hand.
So swift so sure.

He died for me on a
wooden cross so rough.
Nails pierced His flesh.
And yet He did
not mind the pain.
He suffered it all.

The tears they fall,
as I thank Him
on my knees,
for all His bounty.

All of His love.
His greatest gift.
My redeemer.
My saviour.
My all.

Brenda Russell

The Penalty

Love was like a penalty.
You were the goal.
You were my heart.
You were my soul.
I took aim.
I got prepared.
With the thoughts of you.
The times we shared.
I was blind.
I thought love was on my side.
I took the shot.
The ball went wide.
How could I miss.
It's all so weird.
I looked again.
The goal had disappeared.
Why did this happen.
It is so unfair.
But in my heart.
The goal was never there.

James Hibbeler

Text Craze

The screen is empty now,
My love must be asleep.
No little envelope
to sweep me off my feet.

Reflecting on the day gone by,
our words made us reach the sky.
Tomorrow will be another day,
with plenty loving things to say.

But still I stare at the screen
with hope that's true.
When suddenly the words appear
I love you!

    Chandra

Brothers

A brother hugging his brother
A sight so rarely seen
Bag in hand was one departing
Or perhaps had he just been.

I couldn't tell delight or distress
Their precious moment, mine to witness.
This embrace in the street too immediate
For seclusion of lounge or hall.
Had a brother returned from Australia or court
Surely it wasn't just ~ football.

Two brothers' arms round each other
United in joy or despair
Was it marriage or becoming a father
That made this moment to share.

Little did they know it was shared with me
Standing across the street.
This wave of love that flowed from them
And landed at my feet.

Sue Knott

Sisters

Sisters who needs,
some people hate their sisters and never want to see them again.
But me, I love mine.
And enjoy spending each and every day with her,
we argue and fight like other sisters,
But we have a bond that puts things right,
I like being the oldest,
as I'm there if she's in trouble,
or ever needs help.
She'll do the same for me one day,
At the minute she's too young to understand.
I'll always stand by her whatever she's done,
I'm here like a friend or a best mate,
if she ever needs a shoulder to cry on.
So one day when I'm in trouble and need help,
I'll pray and hope that she will do the same,
so in a way we're not just sisters
We're mates as well.
She's my only sister,
I think that's why I love her so much,
it's just her and me.

Laura Perkins

Pepperland

Out where the sun has no pity,
Let's take a trip to Liverpool city,
Where once again,
Listen to the refrain,
Of 'Strawberry Fields' and 'Penny Lane',
There stands the Cavern Club,
Its walls wet with tears,
The day they sank the yellow sub,
What made John Lennon cry,
The day Mark Chapman told him he must die,
Now George Harrison, has gone,
And we are bereft
Only two of 'The Fab Four' are left,
The 'Long and Winding Road'
Has gone into overload,
'Please, Please Me'
Pepperland's without 'Eleanor Rigby'
The sixties filled us with elation,
LSD and meditation,
The Beatles were the heart of the nation,
'All Things Must Pass'
And alas,
George has gone west
As has Epstein and Pete Best,
'Sgt Pepper's Lonely Hearts Club Band'
Is the best in all the land,
And in a hundred years from now,
Or my name's not Alan Pow,
They'll still be humming Beatles tunes,
When we are all dust and bones,
The Beatles shall outlive their gravestones.

Alan Pow

Weary World

Oh! weary world, of war and woe
Mankind's troubles grow and grow
Futile wars that solve nothing
Only misery and hatred bring
Displaced people, travelling to and fro
Searching for somewhere to live and grow
Anger, crime and poverty, fill our city streets
While others boast of their financial feats
Oh! weary world what have we done
Fame and fortune, just for some, but alas, not everyone

Marguerita Johnstone

The Little Colleen

'Please take me back to Ireland,' the little colleen cried
'I want to see my homeland once more before I die.'
She was a new bride on the day that she left
And the loss that she felt was worse than death
Standing on the ferry as she bid goodbye
To the land that held her heart
The sweet green grass she played in as a child
The green fields and the shamrock growing wild
The cutting of the peat and the fires piled high
The fiddle and the harp and the dances and reels
And the oh so sweet music bringing tears to the eyes
The old whitewashed cottage with the roses around the door
How she ached to see it just once more
She longed to see her mother now feeble with age
With hair that was gold and now grey
And her gentle smile as she sat in her old rocking chair
She remembered her pain and the tears that she cried
And that day long ago when she said her goodbyes
'Please take me back to Ireland,' the little colleen cried
'I want to see my homeland once more before I die.'

Christine Isaac

Memories Of Love

My day begins with the memory of you
The touch of magic that was ecstasy
I love, live, breathe your body
Kiss, caress and take you into me

The dawn is breaking and I want you so much
But someone else will be feeling your touch
Yet I must feel no jealousy
Because I am only your fantasy

I lived a whole life in eight perfect hours
My dormant heart awoke with your kiss
I didn't need the hearts and flowers
Just that love that was so briefly ours . . .

Pamela Baily

Autumn

Oh, that I, but could convey
What autumn means to me
To see the glowing colours
Of every bush and tree.

The magic of it all
Never fails to fill me with awe
The bracken so russet
The berries, some blue, some red
The woodlands, with their vivid coloured carpets spread.

The sunlight filtering through the trees
Turning to pure gold, every shining leaf
For me, all this sheer beauty is pure bliss
Knowing, our creator has fashioned all this.

Erika Rollinson

For Matty 'Pon Angel's Wing . . .
(Dedicated to Matthew Carey
who lost his brave fight against leukaemia aged just 15)

One so young tho' still summoned by God;
To that heaven of heavens, the ultimate quest.
High above our heads where angels play, to
beyond the clouds, when called to rest.

To be of faith and sure, of one's self,
tho' why he's taken, we'll never know;
But gone he has and left all, so sad, but, life does go on
tho' Matty left, unable to conquer that nagging foe . . .

. . . no tears are spill'd now, tho' such feelings not in vain;
and but tho' in this, a merciful release, we knoweth
Matty suffers not, no more that pain.

He lived his life, as best tho' disease was constant,
but life he played and yes, almost to the full,
when finally came that usherance for Matty to leave us
as God stopped the pushing and decided now, to pull;

Oh dear Matty, will you ever know
how such feelings and raw emotion ran so for you?
And these tears, all for you, as God intended it to be,
then thoughts, and eyes alofted their gaze to that heaven, to you . . .

. . . and left missed now are you when the sun surely rises on
                                                                         the morning,
testament of your bravery cometh the hour, your smile a joy to see
when all seemed lost, a smile despite the pain, you were suffering . . .

And we miss that smile;
Then come those tears a'tumbling like a mountain spring,
you had been so happy if only a little while in God's creation,
                                                                         but memories
stay and we'll remember, while you fly, 'pon angel's wing . . .

    Ron Matthews Jr

One Year On
(Dedicated to Joyce)

It's now been 365 days
And in all ways
They have been good
No more solitude
In our lives, or our dreams
For it seems
It was meant to be
Fait acompli

It's been 12 months no less
Unhurried progress
Partnership to last
Oblivious to the past
We built again, we began anew
Soft feelings grew
From a tender kiss
What moment this

It's now 1 short year on
Hours passed, time gone
I wouldn't change anything
Because you bring
That love I cherish and need
Fresh hearts indeed
For there's no shame
Returning the same.

George S Johnstone

Bosom Friend

Reached the age of sixty-five years
Had some laughs, seen a few tears
Walked many miles, travelled afar
Occasionally wandering into a bar
Pontificating on the world's demise
Opinions causing no big surprise
An armchair expert on most sports
Unselfish provider of advice and reports
Many times, dogged by rumour
Of not possessing a sense of humour
Too busy to notice, as life rushed by
How green the grass, blue the sky
With good fortune, an occasional pill
The future now is all downhill
Enjoying life without regret
Before disappearing, into the sunset

Albert W Day

Dedicated To Poppy

She was a pet in the full sense
A canine friend with no pretence.
A loving member of the family
A 'lady' of full pedigree.

She was a 'bitch' by birth but not by nature.
A true-blue breed; a loveable creature.
To know her was to love her
A bouncy bundle of fur.

At the end her pain intense.
Her body left with no defence.
A stroke, a fit, a growth all came.
Blind and deaf ~ Oh what a shame.

We do not believe in euthanasia
But in such agony we couldn't see her.
A quick injection ended her pain.
So sad ~ we'll not see her again.

No moist nose inside my shoe.
No more that welcome bark I knew.
No more my hand will stroke her head.
No more her weight at the foot of the bed.

   Goodbye dear friend
    This is the end.

Den Evans

A Tribute To Jackie

Pioneer airplane pilot Jacqueline Cochran
Started flying at the age of thirty in nineteen thirty-two,
First woman to participate in the McRobertson
London-Melbourne Race span,
Winner of the Bendix Trophy Race, too.
This cosmetics firm owner during World War II
Dedicated herself to helping the effort,
Organized and commanded the WASPS ~
Women's Airforce Service Pilots ~ to support
The men in the regular US Air Force.
First civilian woman to receive the
Distinguished Service Award,
Elected to the National Aviation Hall of Fame,
Recognized as an outstanding reward.
Then and now men and women train the same
At Lackland Air Force base ~
For various duties wherever they're sent,
To serve their country ~ time well spent
Giving up freedoms they protect for freedom's sake
Even when their lives are at stake.
A tribute to Jackie and other veterans,
Brave women who enlist in the US WAF.

Flossie

The Tangled Web

I should have walked away
The first time that we met
But like a magnet draws
I was drawn in to the net
Then felt that I was hypnotised
As you weaved your tangled web
The sad thing is I believed those lies
Those lies I came to dread.

A tangled web of deceit
That mesmerized from the start
I was so taken in
And listened with my heart
Then the web became transparent
As clear as it could be
You were only fooling yourself
But that you couldn't see.

Sheila Graham

My Love Forever

Ignited by a spark from eternity
A fire deep within me burns.
The fire of love, that was kindled
The day our lives were joined.

When the last petal has fallen,
And summer is at its end,
My love for you will still be
As a fragrant rose, in full bloom.

When crisp autumn leaves carpet the ground,
And fading light brings shorter days,
The springtime of our love
Will be forever in my heart.

When winter frost dulls the senses,
And we withdraw into a cocoon of memories
I shall still love you,
For the years cannot decay
That, in which time had no part.

J Thompson

Lost Love

I lie on this bed in a vast domain
as moonlight comes shining upon me at night.
Still holding a pillow you fell fast asleep
just like a child but now I must weep
because you have gone. I'm stretching myself,
lying where you lay, while I start to pray,
your living eyes greeting me down the past years.

I rise and stand up by the window but
I'm lonely as waves which won't reach the shore
and clouds drifting by which are making me cry.
The thought of your name makes me gaze outside
at stars bringing tears for the love of past years.
Now nothing and no one can ever be known.
I only see imprints of somebody there.

I think of our parting not so long ago
which made you stop nursing our fragile love.
A touchy ghost stumbles right into my heart
just friendly starlit by passing of time.
We spoke through necessity; loved with your fist.
You now have departed at such a high cost
that now I am looking for paths we have lost.

Nancy Reeves

Lilias Day

Lilias Day was the day when
As a child I ran away
Chasing laughter, children's footsteps
All I knew was I wanted to join them

On I sped along the green and
For a while, was not to be seen
Merrily I spent the day
Among the stalls and people I played

Between the horses and parades
The floats and costumes coloured gay
To see the Queen of Lilias Day
Crowned in all her glory

Away from the noisy, moving throng
I knew I'd find my way back home
Then I got the chance to explore
The float made by the street next door

And there I stayed 'til coming of night
When ~ spotted by neighbours searching ~
Mother fetched me by her side.

Tracy Patrick

An Ode To Margaret

I wrote a poem called Margaret
For me it was a thrill
For I loved her when I wrote it
Indeed I love her still.

It was published first in early June
I was proud to see my name
It was shown in the local papers
It reached such high acclaim.

It was published in America
I was proud of my success
To see it in the magazine
Of owing mills, no less.

They came and took my photograph
With Margaret by my side
The way we stood ten years ago
When she became my bride.

It's now been published eleven times
Which isn't bad so far
But I am just the man with pen
And 'Margaret' is the star.

David Livingstone

Now

Past Errol Flynn's house
Under an old railway tunnel
Terraced streets
The site of town walls
Now a multi-storey car park
Pens of the cattlemarket
Now a superstore.

Paul Wilkins

Huskies In The Snow

Through the mountain pass
The sleek huskies went.
Cutting the packed ice brittle as glass
Fleet-footed, fresh, not spent.
Come, huskies
Come, huskies
Across the snow
Leap!

Through the wind in a whirl
Fighting, exciting, their call.
The sledge gave a dangerous twirl.
The cold it was biting in a heavy snowfall.
Leap huskies
Leap huskies
It's a long way
To go!

Snowed-over as never before
The river was frozen late that year.
The team-driver hugged the shore
While startled onlookers cowered in fear.
Across ice
Cracking ice
The huskies sank in the snow
So confident they were just a moment ago!

Angus Richmond

Benidorm's Not For Me

It's time to turn over a new leaf
From season to season
From summer to winter
It's autumn
And I love it
Always will

Back to playing in the park with friends
like some little Rupert Bear
in woolly jumper and scarf,
we're kicking up the leaves
and then chancing braver adventures
and daring to disturb those swept
under a tree. Anyone looking?
Those friends go abroad now
to lie in the sun and relax
but give me a trip through the valley
along the banks of the Tyne
through tracks that are red and golden
and woods that are mellow and brown
Wonderful!

Mary says my face is glowing
as she serves the morning tea.
A brisk walk into work has done that,
no make-up, just crisp morning air.
And the nights just as sharp yet so cosy,
pull the curtains, settle down and just dream.
Festivals and celebrations are happening,
take a turnip, bag of carrots, or blackberry jam.
And who's that knocking, trick or treating?
Where have I put those sweets?
Still to come sparkling fires and soaring
rockets beneath glowing starry skies.
Magic!

Mary says the nights are drawing in and that's
o'k by me. I'll put the milk out on the step for
Mr Hedgehog, rustling somewhere on the lawn.
Leaves are swirling then they're lifting, you just
can't fence them in. Off to more adventures,
before winter frosts begin.
Who needs a package deal?
Yes, it's autumn and I love it.

Val Stephenson

Dream Spirit

He knew that he had lost her
and nevermore would see her lovely face
or hear her soft sweet voice and gaze
into dark, deep, enigmatic eyes.
Those lovely eyes now hidden 'neath
closed lids, long lashes laid
upon her marble cheeks.
The lovely lips bow curved
as if in secret mirth.

And though the endless years
grind on in waking agony.
They pass, as in a flash, when, in his dreams,
he meets his love and walks with her,
amongst the trees, along the scented paths,
or lies upon the soft meadow grass, outstretched
yet hand in hand. Her gentle touch
a fleeting memory of joy.
Until he wakes again ~ to pain.

D G W Garde

Who Takes The Blame?

Does love not darken my doorstep, to shelter me from pain?
Are a politician's tears only for his own gain?
Is a hero's life full of shame?
And if so then who takes the blame?
Are poets' words just words in a book?
Is life just a mirror to which no one will look?
Is war for our sake? Are we so naive?
And is it not God's book that we believe?
If not then who will relieve?

And as the organ grinders, organ grinds, and the monkeys jump
with death in mind, their guns held high, their thoughts surpressed
Kill, kill, kill we're losing God's test.
Are we not human?
Do we not care?
And as for God I know He's still there, watching all that we do,
and on judgement day we'll pay our due.
But I have to ask, I need to know, if all of this is really so,
and on judgement day if we are punished, and God decides
that life on earth is hell enough and sends us back, would we call
His bluff?

God knows who's to blame, the men who shed no blood and feel no
pain, God knows these men are the ones to blame.
But as for your naiveté and ignorance, and your need to be told
what to do, then God looks at you with judging eyes too.
And at the end of it all, when we all lye still, and the scores
on each side will read, *nil-nil.*
Who takes the blame for the waste of land? For the blisters on
the grave digger's hand?
For the children left, who'll make their stand?
Who'll feel the shame?
Who'll take the blame?

Nicola Esther Pearson

Yesterday
(Dedicated to September 11, 2001)

you thought tomorrow would
bring light ~
those quiet shadowed footfalls
could cease following

today is almost gone
& you can feel the tension
grinding through your teeth
& taste the iron on your tongue

while yesterday's smoke lingers ~
tearing eyes & choking lungs
today's smoldering passions ignite
& pieces coalesce a oneness

as the planet Earth rotates
on its axis of despair & in its
orbit of deception ~ just look
at yonder darkening horizon

global storm clouds gathering
hemispherical lightning strikes as rains
of terror tumble from the skies ~ I pray
there is no tomorrow like yesterday

Edward L Smith & Carmen M Pursifull

Lost Friends . . .

Where are all those friends, where have they all gone to?
I sometimes wish that they were here
To share an ecstasy or two,
To cordial meetings and of lively cheer,
Only pleasant circumstances, with little else to fear.

There was Uncle George and Uncle Fred,
    and that assortment of funny aunts,
Who insisted on being at every village dance.
I can remember the vicar's Sunday sermon,
We reposed and pondered on every mortal theme,
And later running along to Aunt Lil's for ripe
    strawberries and extra thick cream.

Where ever are those nieces and long lost cousins
And kindly Edith and her audacious and wearisome sons?
. . . And Margaret, Mary and eloquent Sue,
Oh! and not forgetting Martha too.

The uproarious company, I should say, are long departed,
Though I writhe not in melancholy nor feel downhearted,
With silent spells being broken only by a shrouded sigh.
Bu I shall be ever grateful, you see,
For all those little things that they did for me.

    Michael F Bullock of Alltsaigh

VOICES OF TODAY

poetry Pt today